ARTIST TRANSCRIPTIONS
SAXOPHONE
Transcribed by TODD NYSTROM

The Best Of K

CW00531436

MONTAGE

G. FORCE

ISBN 0-7935-3054-7

HAL•LEONARD™
CORPORATION

7777 W. BLUEMOUND RD. P.O. BOX 13819 MILWAUKEE, WI 53213

Against Doctor's Orders

By Kenny G, Preston Glass and Alan Glass

E
A. Sax
Synth. Pads
Aux. Synth.
Kybd. Bass
Gtr.
Elec. Bass
Drums Perc.
G7sus
G7
E♭maj9
C/F
G7
C/G
G7sus
G7
fill

Esther

By Kenny G

17

G Force

By Kenny G, McClain and Sause

Going Home

By Kenny G and Walter Afanasieff

Home

By Kenny G

40

I've Been Missing You

By Kenny G and Kashif

48

Japan

By Kenny G and Randy Jackson

Last Night Of The Year

By Kenny G and Peter Scherer

Midnight Motion

By Kenny G

Sade

By Kenny G

Silhouette

By Kenny G

Songbird

By Kenny G

Tradewinds

By Kenny G

Tribeca

By Kenny G, Kashif and Wayne Brathwaite